# MYSTERIES & MARVELS OF BIRD LIFE

## Ian Wallace, Rob Hume and Rick Morris

### Edited by Rick Morris
with Marit McKerchar

### Designed by Teresa Foster,
Anne Sharples, Sally Godfrey,
Lesley Davey and Polly Dawes

### Illustrated by David Quinn,
Alan Harris, David Mead,
Wayne Ford and Ian Jackson

### Cartoons by John Shackell

First published in 1984
by Usborne Publishing Ltd, 20 Garrick Street,
London WC2E 9BJ.
© 1984 by Usborne Publishing Ltd.

The name Usborne and the device ⬤ are Trade Marks
of Usborne Publishing Ltd.

Printed in Great Britain

# Contents

The Quetzal, from Central America, was worshipped by the Aztecs as "the god of the air".

To avoid damaging his long feather train, the male drops backwards off his perch before flying away. When he sits on the eggs the train pokes up to 30 cm out of the nest hole.

The colourful but balding King Vulture from the rainforests of Central and South America. It is probably one of the few birds to find its food by smell.

2

Long-tailed Widow
Bird from Africa.

# About this book

There are more than 8,600 species of
birds and new species are still being
found. In total, about 100,000 million
birds are flying, walking or swimming
around the world. They can be seen in
coal mines and on mountain tops, in
jungles, cities and deserts, and over
oceans and icecaps. Almost wherever you
look you will see birds. This book is
a lively introduction to many of the
species and concentrates on the more
curious and unexpected parts of their
varied lives.

　　Birds range in size from smaller
than moths to taller than people. Some
are great travellers, literally flying
around the world. Others cannot fly at
all. This book looks at birds that
dance, vegetarian vultures, birds that
fly backwards, bone-eaters, parrots
that sleep upside down, a heron that
fishes with bait, and a poorwill that
sleeps through the winter.

　　This book reveals the fascination
and beauty of birds and shows that
there is still much to learn about
the way they live.

Prince
Rudolph's
Blue Bird
of Paradise
has a
brilliant
upside-down
display.

To attract a
female the Sage
Grouse puffs out
chest air sacs and
displays his
spiked tail
feathers.

The Cock-of-the-
Rock displays in
the jungles of
Surinam,
South
America.

The
Australian
Tawny
Frogmouth
looks like
a broken
branch.

Young Tawny
Frogmouth.

Roseate
Spoonbill

It sifts
food with
its beak.

**TRUE or FALSE?**

Look out for these
questions and try to
guess if they are
true or false. The
answers are on p.32.

# Fabulous feathers

Birds are not the only animals which fly – bats and insects also do. But birds are the only animals with feathers. Feathers keep them warm and help them to stay up in the air. Their colours may be used in courtship or as camouflage.

Worn feather in spring.

Brown tip in autumn.

## Turning black ▶

The wear on feathers can change a bird's colours. In his new autumn plumage, the male Black Lark of Asia is mottled brown. As wear removes the feathers' pale brown tips, black patches appear. By the spring, he is totally jet black and ready to court a female.

Autumn

Spring

Male Black Lark of Asia

## Long ones ▶

Many birds grow long feathers on their head, tail or wings.

When displaying to females, the King of Saxony Bird of Paradise raises his two head plumes and bounces about on branches.

Each plume is 60 cm long

African Snipe "drumming".

Male King of Saxony Bird of Paradise

## ◀ Musical feathers

The African Snipe dives steeply through the air when he displays over his breeding site. As he dives, he makes a bleating "hoo-oo-oo-oo-oo-oo-ooh" sound, known as "drumming". This noise is produced by the air passing through stiff tail feathers which are spread out on each side.

Ruby-throated Hummingbird

## Feather facts

The Whistling Swan has over 25,000 feathers. The much smaller Pied-billed Grebe has far denser plumage, with 15,000 feathers. The tiny Ruby-throated Hummingbird has only 940 but still has more feathers per square centimetre than the swan.

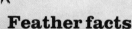

Whistling Swan

Pied-billed Grebe

**Pygmy Sunbird**

The long tail feathers of the Pygmy Sunbird help it to turn quickly when flying.

Herons have no less than five powder puffs, one on the chest and two on each thigh.

Male nightjar displaying plumes to female.

**Male**

African tribesmen call this nightjar "the bird with four wings". It only has two wings but has an amazingly long display feather on each one.

Comb on one claw.

Standard-winged Nightjars

Blue-crowned Motmot

Racket →

The Blue-crowned Motmot pulls feather barbs from its tail to leave two racket-shaped feathers.

**Female**

## Powder and comb▲

Some birds have special powder puffs which they use to groom their feathers. Herons clean off fish slime by rubbing their feathers through the powder. A comb on one of their claws removes the clogged powder and leaves the feathers clean and tidy.

Layers of transparent horn on the "eye" produce the dazzling colours.

## ◄ A brown tale

A peacock's wonderful train of feathers is actually brown. The shining colours of the "eyes" are due to layers of horn which reflect and bend light.

The peacock has a fairly short tail hidden under the colourful train.

## Not really bald

The feathers of the American Bald Eagle are quite heavy. They make up one sixth of its total weight.

# Eating out

Birds have no hands, so they have to find their food with their beaks and feet.

## Fishing bait ▶

Most herons wait patiently to catch fish but the Green Heron uses bait to attract them. It creeps to the water's edge with an insect caught for the purpose and drops it into the water. It then waits, completely still, for small fish to come to the bait. If the insect drifts away, the heron fetches it and puts it back in position.

Green Heron

Placing the insect . . .

. . . waiting . . .

. . . and a swift strike of the bill catches the fish.

The top of the bill is 5 cm long.

## Chisel and spear ▶

A honeycreeper from Hawaii, the Akiapolaau, has a unique bill for finding food in the wood of dead trees. The top of the bill is long and curved, and the bird lifts this up while using the shorter, chisel-like bottom to pound into the tree. It spears the disturbed insects and larvae with the top of the bill.

The Limpkin even feeds snails to its young.

The Everglades Kite feeds only on snails.

## Snail snacks

A water snail of the Florida swamps is the speciality of two birds. The Limpkin, with its long legs and bill, wades after snails, searching for them on underwater plants. The Everglades Kite — an odd bird of prey — must wait for the snails to come near the surface in the cool of the day. The kite snatches them up with its feet and flies to a branch. Its hooked beak prises the snail from the shell.

TRUE or FALSE?

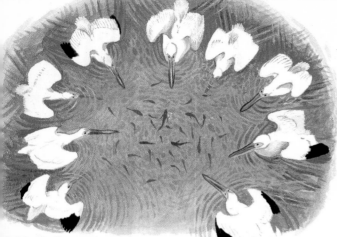

## Fish herders ▲

Up to 40 White Pelicans gather together in a horseshoe formation to "herd" fish into shallow water. Beating their wings and feet, they drive the fish before them. Every 15-20 seconds, as though at a signal, they plunge their bills into the centre of the arc and scoop up the trapped fish. About one in every five plunges is successful. Each pelican eats roughly 1,200 grammes of fish a day.

White
Pelicans

The huge pouch makes an excellent fishing net. It shrinks to squeeze out the water before the fish is swallowed.

## A nutty larder ▼

The Acorn Woodpecker lives in small flocks in American oak woods. It harvests acorns and, if available, almonds and walnuts as well. In autumn it stores the nuts tightly in holes in the trees — so tightly that squirrels cannot pull them out. The woodpecker drills the holes with its beak and will re-use them year after year. The stored acorns are emergency winter food for the little 20-24 cm woodpecker.

### Teaspoon effect

Grey
Phalarope

To create whirlpools, the Grey Phalarope swims in tight circles and spins its body around. This has the same effect as stirring coffee with a teaspoon. Small animals in the water are probably drawn into the centre of the whirlpool where the phalarope can catch them.

Acorn
Woodpecker

Squirrel trying to steal acorns.

The woodpeckers share their acorns but drive away birds from other flocks.

The Harpy Eagle eats monkeys for breakfast.

On mild days it catches insects in mid-air — most unusual for a woodpecker.

# Pirates and scavengers

Most birds find their own food but some have ways of stealing it from others. Birds are also good scavengers and are always on the lookout for an easy meal.

## The early bird . . .

Flocks of Lapwings and Golden Plovers feed together on worms they pull from the ground. Black-headed Gulls join these flocks and steal the worms if they can. Lapwings are the gulls' favourite targets because they take longer to pull out the worms and are less agile when chased.

The gulls may repay the plovers by warning them of predators.

Black-headed Gull

Golden Plover

Lapwing

Arctic Tern

Arctic Skuas eat small mammals, birds, eggs and insects. Stolen fish is their main diet.

Arctic Skua

Sand Eel

Skuas catch the disgorged meal in mid-air.

## Marine pirates ▲▼

The Arctic Skua is a graceful pirate which chases other seabirds to make them disgorge their catch of fish. The speed and agility of a pair of skuas when pursuing a gull or tern is amazing. In areas where the large Great Skua is common, the smaller Arctic Skua chases Arctic Terns, Kittiwakes and Puffins, while the Great Skua goes after Guillemots, Razorbills, Puffins and Gannets.

The Great Skua also pounces on seagulls, drowning them, and steals seabird chicks.

## Truly Magnificent Frigatebird ▼

The Magnificent Frigatebird is a master of the air. It has huge, long wings and a long tail which it uses as a rudder and brake. It never settles on water and is clumsy on land but in the air it is a wonderful flier. Frigatebirds catch flying fish above the waves and feed on young turtles on beaches and fish disgorged by frightened boobies which they chase unmercifully. The way they chase these relatives of the Gannet was described in the log kept by Christopher Columbus.

Female

Male

Magnificent Frigatebird catching a flying fish.

Magnificent Frigatebird chasing a White Booby.

Arctic Skuas will fiercely attack people who come near the nest.

## Ant antics

As columns of army ants march through the forests of South America, they flush out insects, frogs and small mammals. The White-fronted Antbird follows the ant "armies", preying on the escaping creatures. The birds rarely eat the ants.

Lammergeier

## Bone breakers ▲

One vulture, the Lammergeier, has learnt to dispose of skeletons. It picks up a bone, flies very high with it and then drops it on to hard, flat rocks. The vulture eats the bone marrow from the broken pieces or, amazingly, swallows bits of bone. The White-necked Raven also drops bones but often gets its aim wrong and they fall on to grass.

## Eye in the sky ▶

Eiders, Mergansers, Smews and other diving ducks are often watched by Herring Gulls. When they bring up fish and shell-fish, the gulls steal it if they can.

A patrolling Herring Gull, keeping an eye on the ducks.

Female

Male

Eiders diving for mussels. They can dive for over a minute to depths of 20 metres.

TRUE or FALSE?

After bathing, Starlings dry themselves on sheep.

# Staking a claim

To breed successfully, birds need a safe place to build their nests, freedom from disturbance and a good supply of food. They may need to compete with other members of their own species for a suitable territory.

## A reserved table ▼

Shelducks defend a breeding territory and the male also keeps a feeding territory nearby. The female feeds here unchallenged during the brief times she leaves the eggs. When the young hatch, they are led to this feeding area which is already free of other Shelducks who would compete for food.

As the sexes look alike, the male relies on song and display to get the right response from a female.

Robins' summer areas.

breeding territories

nest

winter

feeding

Robins' winter territories are smaller.

## ◀ Seeing red

The Robin's song can be heard clearly all around its territory. This saves it a lot of work patrolling the boundary. In spring the male's song warns off other males but attracts females. The sight of a red breast on his territory sends the male into a fury. He attacks other males or sometimes his own reflection or even a red rag hung in a tree.

Female with her ducklings.

The nest may be some way from the shore, in an old rabbit burrow.

Male Shelduck

breeding territories

feeding

river

Shelduck territories defended by the male.

island

Non-defended feeding area

breeding areas

Australian Gannets

Gannets nest on cliffs and islands.

## ◀ Sharing things

Gannets feed on fish in the sea. There is no point in having an individual feeding territory because they actually benefit from being in flocks, tiring out the fish by diving and chasing. Thousands of Gannets nest together and keep only a tiny territory – as far as a sitting bird can reach – around each nest.

TRUE or FALSE?

Bellbirds chime together.

Wedge-tailed
Eagles

The eagles fight
in mid-air and
on the ground.

Woodpeckers
know their mate's and
neighbour's drumming and
recognise intruders.

## ▲Fighting eagles

Eagles hunt over huge
areas and only defend a
small area around the nest
from other eagles. The
great Wedge-tailed Eagle
of Australia, however,
fights to keep strange
agles out of its whole area.
Eagles may fall to the
ground and be locked in
battle for up to half an
hour. To help avoid such
fights, the eagle performs
territorial displays to
"warn off" the intruder.

Pileated Woodpecker

The defending eagle soars through
he air performing aerobatics.

Male and
female
displaying.

## Drumming
## accents▶

Woodpeckers do not
sing to mark their
territory, but they
drum their beaks against
a tree to produce a loud,
rapid rattle. The birds
can hear enough difference
in the speed and rhythm to
recognise each other.

The Great Grey Owl of northern
Europe and North America has
a wingspan of 150 cm.

## Fearsome defender ▲

The Great Grey Owl defends its nest and
young fearlessly. It will attack
human intruders and can cause serious
wounds. Some skuas, eagles and
other owls also attack people in
defence of their nest.

11

# Wooing a mate

All birds have a strong urge to breed. Finding a fit and loyal mate is all important. Generally the male advertises himself with a song, a loud call or bright plumage to attract a female.

## Turning it on ▶

These striking birds are males trying to impress females. Some, such as Temminck's Tragopan, grow special feathers or fleshy skin for the breeding season. Others reveal hidden markings in their wings.

Sunbittern showing hidden markings

Count Raggi's Bird of Paradise males.

Horns

Temminck's Tragopan — the horns and wattle are colourful flesh which expands.

Wattle

## ◀ Brilliant display

Up to ten males of Count Raggi's Bird of Paradise display together in a tree. Each one clears away leaves that might block out the sun and defends his perch. Loud calls and bright, shimmering feathers attract a drab female. She chooses the male with the most dazzling plumage and most dramatic display. This top bird will mate with many females but the other males will probably not mate at all.

Temminck's Tragopan is a Chinese pheasant

## ◀ Come into my bower

In Australia and New Guinea, male bowerbirds build and decorate a bower to attract a female. Usually, the duller the bird, the more elaborate and decorative his bower. Some collect snail shells or whitened bones, or anything blue, such as flowers, feathers and berries. When the female arrives, the male dances. She inspects him and his bower and they mate. She then builds her nest and rears the chicks on her own.

The Satin Bowerbird paints the inside of his bower with the blue juices from berries, using bark as a paintbrush.

Over 500 bones and 300 snail shells were found on the dance floor of one bower.

## Ruff justice ▲

Ruff males and females are quite different. The larger colourful males display on a grass area known as a lek. Each male tries to hold a small territory, displaying his plumage and defending the area against rival males. Females fly in, select a male and mate. They rear their brood on their own.

Female

Males with dark ruffs attract the most females.

## ▼Song and dance routine

Japanese Cranes "sing" and "dance" when courting. Pairs sing duets, pointing their bills skywards. A single puff of steam rises in the cold air as the male cries "kaar" and two puffs rise as the female replies "ka-ka". They start dancing slowly; bowing, flapping wings and turning circles, then speed up, finally leaping 2-3 metres into the air.

Japanese Cranes

Western Grebes "rushing".

## Walking on water ▶

Weed dance.

Western Grebes perform an amazing water run, rearing up side by side to charge across the water, powered by their splashing feet. Part of their courtship, this "rushing" is a test of breeding fitness. Later, male and female dive together and surface with weed in their bills. In a swimming ballet, they touch breasts and slowly rise up with bills pointing skyward, touching their weed together.

TRUE or FALSE?

Courting pelicans exchange fish.

# Setting up home

Many animals – including mammals, insects and even fish – make some sort of nest. But birds make the most amazing and varied nests to hold their eggs and young.

## ▼ Dad's compost nest

The Mallee Fowl's nest is the largest made by any bird. The male builds a vast mound of soil and fills the egg chambers with damp, rotting plant material. The female lays her eggs inside these chambers and the male covers them over. Like a compost heap, the plant material rots and ferments, creating enough heat to incubate the eggs. The male opens up the chambers to reduce the heat and, at night, covers them with warm sand.

The young birds, which are almost fully feathered, break out of the mound on their own and may never see their parents.

Several thousand pairs of flamingos nest together.

The female sometimes lays 2 eggs.

Mallee Fowl

The male looks after the mound for 9 months.

Mallee Fowl's nest.

The nest is 1 metre deep. The mound over it can be 1 m high and 5 m across.

The male's beak is a "thermometer". It helps him keep the nest at a constant temperature of 33°C.

## Egg cup ▼

The Greater Treeswift glues strips of bark together to make a tiny cup. The cup, on a high branch, is just large enough to hold one egg and is one of the smallest nests in the world.

**TRUE or FALSE?**

Parrots nest with termites.

Greater Treeswift

Fairy Tern

## No nest ▶

The Fairy Tern makes no nest at all. The female lays her one egg in a tiny hollow on a branch or in the fork of two branches. The chick has sharp claws for clinging to the swaying branch which is often high off the ground

Sitting behind the eg adults incubate it wi their breast feather

Nest

## Upstairs, downstairs ▶

The Hammerhead's nest may be up to 2 metres across. It is solidly built of sticks, has a high domed roof and three chambers. The highest and safest from flooding when the nest is low over a river, has three to five eggs. The young soon grow too big and move to the middle chamber. The lowest chamber is an entrance "hall".

Rufous Ovenbird

Hammerhead shooting into the tiny entrance with closed wings.

Building the nest may take six months.

## ◀ Well done

The ovenbirds get their name from their nests, many of which look like native mud ovens. One species builds an extraordinary 3-metre high "block of flats" with several entrances. The Rufous Ovenbird builds a strong mud nest, often perched on top of a fence post. The nest has an entrance tunnel and a separate nesting chamber. It weighs about 9 kg.

Nesting chamber

Tunnel entrance

## ◀ Mud mounds

Flamingos nest in colonies near lakes. Their nests are mounds of mud 40 cm across and up to 45 cm high, with a hollow scoop for the egg at the top. This gave rise to many strange ideas of how the incubating birds sat on their eggs. They actually sit on their legs with their heels poking out under their chests. The mounds last for years.

Pygmy Falcon

The straw thatch is waterproof.

## A busy village ▶

Dozens of Social Weavers make a huge nest together. They build a roof in the top of a tall tree. Under this are nests of straw, each with a tunnel of stiff straws pointing downwards from a round chamber. The nests are used for roosting all the year round and may be occupied for 100 years or more. Many of the chambers may be taken over by other birds, so Social Weavers, Red-headed Finches, Lovebirds and Pygmy Falcons may all live together.

Each pair has its own entrance and nest chamber.

Rosy-Faced Lovebird

Social Weaver

# Eggs to adults

Inside the egg the nervous system and heart of the young bird develop first – then the limbs, body and head, swollen by enormous eyes. When the embryo is fully developed it starts to breathe from an air space inside the shell. To get out of the egg it grows an "egg-tooth" to crack the shell.

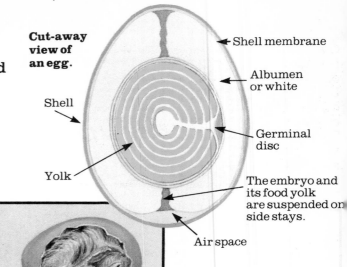

Cut-away view of an egg.

Shell membrane

Albumen or white

Shell

Germinal disc

Yolk

The embryo and its food yolk are suspended on side stays.

Air space

## Chicken's egg

At 3 days the chick's heart already beats. It has blood vessels.

At 15 days the chick is recognisable as a bird.

At 20 days it is fully developed and will hatch next day.

The eggs must be turned regularly by the parents to help the chicks develop properly. This is not easy for the Black-winged Stilt, with its long legs and long beak.

## Egg care ▶

Some birds have one large patch of bare skin (a brood patch) to cover their eggs, while others have separate patches for each egg. The sitting bird leaves the eggs from time to time to stop them getting too hot. Overheating is more of a risk than the cold.

Gamebirds, gulls and waders have separate brood patches.

The Oystercatcher has three brood patches.

## ▼ Hard-working parents

Great Tit with a caterpillar for the young.

All that nestlings want is food, warmth, shelter, and more food. A pair of Great Tits visited their brood with food 10,685 times in 14 days. A female Wren fed her young 1,217 times in 16 hours.

## "Hello, mum" ▶

Several days before hatching, the chick makes peeping calls from inside the egg. The hen replies, so when the chick hatches it already knows its mother's voice. Chicks which leave the nest soon after hatching quickly learn to follow their mother – she becomes "imprinted" on the chick. If they do not see their mother first, something else may become imprinted on them as "mother". Greylag Goose chicks have become attached to people in this way and one even regarded a wheelbarrow as its mother.

**TRUE or FALSE?**

Hungry young eaglets eat their parents.

## A row of owlets ▶

Owls start incubating when the first egg is laid. The later eggs may hatch several days after the first, and the chicks will be different sizes. If the parents cannot catch enough food, the oldest, biggest chicks dominate the others and take it all. That way, one or two chicks survive, which is better than all of them having an equal share of food, and all starving at the same time.

Long-eared Owl

When there is plenty of food all the chicks survive.

Female

Unlike most birds, each female mates with several males.

Each female lays 11-18 eggs.

Male

## Too many eggs

An old male Rhea may attract up to eight hens to his nest. The hens, however, will lay eggs anywhere before the nest is ready and then they will overfill it with 30 or more eggs. The cock cannot cover them all, and the hen may lay more eggs out of his reach. Since the nesting and care of the eggs and young is left entirely to the male, many of the eggs are completely wasted.

One male may incubate as many as 80 eggs.

The scientist, Konrad Lorenz, has acted as "mother" to many geese while studying their behaviour.

Canada Geese and goslings.

## Nursery group ▲

Several adult Canada Geese will often look after the young of other parents. They may be in charge of dozens of goslings. Some ducks also have nursery groups of up to 100.

# Special relationships

To find food and survive, some birds have developed special relationships with other birds, with human beings and other animals. Sometimes this works to the benefit of both but often one takes advantage of the other.

A Peregrine Falcon scaring off an Arctic Fox.

Red-breasted Geese

### ▼ The "cuckoo" duck

The Black-headed Duck is the only duck that copies the cuckoos and lays its eggs in other birds' nests. Unlike young cuckoos, the newly-hatched duck does not push out its companions and only shares their food for a few days before wandering off alone. The duck usually chooses water birds to foster her young but she has been known to lay her eggs in hawks' nests.

Chimango hawk

A Black-headed Duck laying her egg in a Chimango's nest in the Andes.

### The Peregrine connection ▲▶

In the Arctic, Red-breasted Geese know that the presence of Peregrine Falcons means the absence of Arctic Foxes which prey on the geese and their goslings. So they nest within sight and easy reach of the falcon eyries, confident that the Peregrines will chase off the foxes. But as the numbers of falcons have declined, so have the geese.

### ▼ All in the family

White-fronted Bee-eaters of Kenya have a complicated social life. They nest in sand cliffs in colonies of up to 225 pairs. A male must guard his mate closely as a lone female will be quickly mobbed by other males and forced to mate. When food is scarce, dominant males force younger relatives, both male and female, to help feed their chicks. Up to a dozen birds will assist a dominant pair. When this happens, younger birds cannot breed themselves but gain experience for the next year.

## Elder Sisters ▶

Sometimes young birds from a first brood will play "elder sister" to their parents' later broods. Young Moorhens often do this, looking after and feeding one or two broods of younger brothers and sisters. This probably makes them better parents.

A young Moorhen helping the adult with nest repairs.

Cattle Tyrant

Young Moorhen feeding a new chick.

## ◀▼ Easy Rider

Some birds hitch lifts on larger animals and wait for food to be provided by them. In Africa, the Carmine Bee-eater rides the huge Kori Bustard. In South America, the Cattle Tyrant sits on cows. Both watch for flying insects put up by their hosts and then capture them in the air.

Carmine Bee-eater riding on the back of a Kori Bustard.

### TRUE or FALSE?

Blue Drongos help Chinese fishermen.

## Where eagles dare ▼

Since the White-tailed Eagle has been protected, it has become less shy. Many eagles have learnt that fishermen will throw them fish scraps. Returning fishing boats are now followed by gulls, Fulmars and White-tailed Eagles.

White-tailed Eagle

Fulmar

Gulls

Arctic Fox

# Colourful characters

Birds use colour in displays against rival males and to attract mates. Bright colours also attract predators, so some birds only show off their colours in display, and some are only coloured during the mating season. Females, who normally guard the eggs, are generally duller than the males, but this is not always so.

Neck cape pulled out to reveal markings.

Male Lady Amherst's Pheasant

## Mating mask ▼

During the mating season, the Tufted Puffin's normally sober appearance undergoes a complete change. He wears coloured "spectacles", a brightly coloured bill, and golden head plumes like overgrown eyebrows. The Puffin uses its bill for "billing" in courtship — the male and female rub bills together.

Tufted Puffins "billing".

The Tufted Puffin is much duller in winter.

## Lady's man ▲▶

Male Lady Amherst's Pheasants have a glorious plumage, as do most cock pheasants. The female, though, is a dull mottled brown which gives her excellent camouflage amongst scrub, bamboo thickets and woods. During courtship the male prances around the female, spreading his feathers to show his brilliant colours to their best advantage.

## ▼ Snipe's stripes

The Jack Snipe uses the stripes which run along its body to give it perfect camouflage in the marshes where it lives. When it lands, it turns its body, so that the stripes go in the same direction as the surrounding vegetation.

Jack Snipe

The bird remains quite still when its body is in the correct position.

Male frigatebird

## TRUE or FALSE?

The Booby's feet are blue with cold.

Toco Toucan

The beak is very light but strong. Serrated edges, like teeth, slice through its food.

The 23 cm beak is as long as its body.

## Colour collection ▶

The Lesser Flamingo's delicate colour is thought to come from chemicals, called cartenoids, in its food. Flamingos in zoos may lose their colour if not fed on the right diet. The flamingo filters algae from the water through bristles in its bill.

Lesser Flamingo

## Beautiful beaks ▲

The brilliant colours and size of the toucan's beak are a mystery. The toucan uses its beak to reach for fruit, duel with rival males and to scare small birds in order to eat their eggs, but there appears to be no reason for the beak to be quite so colourful.

## ▼ Fabulous females

For a long time, scientists thought that the male and female Red-lined Parrot were males of two separate species because they look so different. Both are very colourful but, surprisingly, the female is more striking than the male. In addition to the bright plumage, its noisy cries announce its presence in the jungle.

## ▼ Balloon bird

The male frigatebird attracts his mate with an amazing wobbly "balloon", which is an inflated throat sac. During the display he vibrates his wings and makes gobbling noises. The female shows her consent by nibbling his feathers and she rubs her head on the "balloon".

Male

Female

The Red-lined Parrot feeds on fruits, berries and nuts.

Frigatebirds nest in bushes and trees.

They live in Australia and New Guinea.

# Migration marvels

Each spring, many birds fly from their winter grounds to summer breeding areas. Some species fly thousands of kilometres on this migration. After breeding they return to their winter areas where the food supply will be more plentiful.

Bar-headed Geese

## Over the top

Bar-headed Geese fly from central Asia over the Himalayas – the world's highest mountain range – to reach their winter grounds in north India and Burma. The flight takes the birds up to an amazing height of 8,000 m – almost as high as cruising jet planes.

## Moon and mud myths ▶

Before scientists discovered the facts of bird migration, people had some amazing ideas to explain where birds went in winter. Swallows were believed to dive into ponds and sleep in the mud at the bottom until spring. Some people thought birds went to the moon. Others thought small birds, like Goldcrests, hitched lifts on large birds such as storks.

Having left its breeding areas around the Bering Straits, there are few places to stop before the bird reaches the Hawaiian islands.

Bristle-thighed Curlews

## Dots in the ocean ▶

The accuracy of some migrations is astonishing. For millions of years, Bristle-thighed Curlews from Alaska have wintered about 9,000 km away on tiny islands in the Pacific Ocean. To reach Hawaii or Tahiti they fly south on a bearing of 170°, continually altering course to allow for winds which drift them off target.

# Migration mystery

House Martins are common summer breeders in Europe but where do they go in winter? They winter in Africa but no one is quite sure where. Many thousands have been ringed in the UK but so far only one has been recovered. In 1984 a ringed House Martin was found in Nigeria. Do all UK House Martins winter in Nigeria?

House Martins from European countries seem to winter in different parts of Africa. Birds from Germany have been found in Uganda.

## Fast flight ▲

A Knot ringed in England took only eight days to reach Liberia, 5,600 km away. Its average speed was 29 km/h.

African Fish Eagle

Tawny Eagle

## Social seasons ▶

The Turtle Dove is common in the woods and farmlands of Europe in summer. In winter it travels to Africa and roosts in huge flocks. One roost was shared with 50 Tawny Eagles, 15 Fish Eagles and hundreds of Black Kites — strange company for a bird whose summer neighbours are Chaffinches and Blackbirds.

Black Kites

Turtle Doves

Its temperature drops to 13°C and its heart beats very slowly.

The Poorwill crawls into a sheltered hole, fluffs out its feathers, and settles for a long, deep sleep.

## Deep sleep

The Poorwill of western North America stays put during the winter months. It copes with the hardest months, when food is scarce, by hibernating. (The Trilling Nighthawk is the only other bird found hibernating.) Before hibernating, it builds up a store of fat which it can live on. About 10 grams of fat is enough "fuel" for 100 days.

It eats as much as possible before going to sleep.

23

# The ultimate fliers

Most birds fly and are great masters of the air. Their powers of flight are matched only by the finest of the insect fliers.

The 9 cm-long Ruby-throated Hummingbird migrates over 3,000 km. 800 km is over the Gulf of Mexico.

## World's worst flier?

The tinamou flies off at breakneck speed but lacks control and may kill itself by crashing headlong into a tree. Speed soon exhausts it and, if flushed from its perch several times, it can become too tired to fly. Tinamous have been seen to dash half way across a river and then flutter down to the water, tired out. Fortunately, they swim quite well and so may reach the bank. Even when running, these birds sometimes stumble and fall.

## The tiniest ◄ helicopter

Hummingbirds are not only quick and agile in forward flight, they can fly up, down, sideways, backwards and upside down. As well as this they can hover perfectly keeping their bills quite still as they suck nectar from flowers. Their narrow wings beat 20-50 times a second and one species has been recorded at 90 beats a second. The Bee Hummingbird (males are only 57mm long) is smaller and lighter than some hawk moths.

Hovering

Flying backwards

Great Dusky Swift

Beginning to roll

## Swift flowing ►

Great Dusky Swifts nest and roost on cliffs behind waterfalls and must fly through sheets of falling water. Occasionally they are swept away by a sudden torrent but usually manage to struggle free.

Swept-back wings and a torpedo-shaped body are a superb design for speed.

Swifts fly in their sleep.

TRUE or FALSE?

Oilbird

## Flying Potholers ▲

The amazing Oilbird of South America
lives completely in the dark. At night,
working by smell, it eats fruit from
forest trees. By day it roosts in dark
hill caves where it also nests. To find
their nests and roosts, they use
echo-location, giving out clicks and
getting back echoes from solid
objects. The echoes can be easily
heard by the human ear.

## Air display mystery

Starling flocks and flocks of small
waders, like Dunlins, have remarkable
co-ordination in the air. They twist,
turn and change direction almost as
one. No one knows how such perfect
harmony is achieved amongst
thousands of birds.

Starlings at dusk.

## ◀Riding the thermals

The Andean Condor is the
heaviest bird of prey and
has the largest wing area
of any bird. Its huge wings —
often over three metres from
tip to tip — are perfect for
soaring. It glides over
mountains for hours, on
updraughts of warm air
(thermals), searching
for carrion to eat.

Andean Condors
weigh over 10kg.

As it hovers, a hummingbird's
wings twist into the shape
of a propeller
and the wingtips
move in a figure-
of-eight to give
perfect control.

Forward
flight

Rolling over

Upside down

Forward
upside down

Turning over

Ruby-throated
Hummingbird

**25**

# Sprints and marathons

As well as flying, most birds walk, run or hop. Those which depend most on their legs and feet are the ones which have lost the power to fly. Feet are also a source of power for waterbirds.

## Running on water ▶

No bird can actually walk on water but the African Jacana comes close. With toes and claws up to eight centimetres long, it can stalk or sprint over thinly scattered marsh plants with no risk of sinking. Its other name is Lily-trotter.

The African Jacana can fly, swim or dive if it has to.

Ostriches have been trained to herd sheep and to scare birds from crops.

Adelie Penguins

Greater Roadrunner

Running circles around a rattlesnake, the Roadrunner darts in and out, dodging the fangs and tiring out the snake.

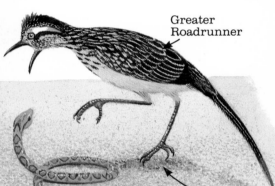

At the right moment, it dashes in and hammers its bill against the snake's head to kill it.

## ◀ Beep, beep! ▼

The Roadrunner of North America is a member of the cuckoo family. It is a poor flier and is best on the ground, running long distances, sprinting, zigzagging and darting nimbly between obstacles. It reaches speeds of 40 km/h, and is faster than any Olympic athlete. A cunning hunter, it will sprint out of cover and catch swifts flying down to drink from desert pools.

The Roadrunner swallows the dead snake whole. It may be seen running around with the snake's tail hanging from its bill.

## ◀ Long legs

The flightless Ostrich can be up to 2.7 metres tall with legs over 1.2 metres long. These are the longest and most powerful legs of any bird. The Ostrich can easily run at 45 km/h for 15-20 minutes and sprint at more than 70 km/h. Ostriches are nomads, joining in the game migrations of Africa to graze hundreds of kilometres of grassland.

The Ostrich only has two toes.

An Ostrich's kick can kill a man.

Sanderling

## ◀ On its toes

All wading birds are nimble but the Sanderling moves so fast along the water's edge that it no longer grows a hind toe. It tilts forward and dashes about on its three front toes.

Impeyan Pheasant

Snow Leopard

## ◀ Penguin marathons

Penguins cannot fly. To reach their Antarctic breeding grounds, Adelie Penguins waddle for up to 320 kilometres over ice floes and snow-covered rocks. When the sun is out, they march steadily in the right direction, but when it is cloudy they seem to lose their way.

## ▲ Hill walker

All pheasants fly only short distances because they lack the normal ability of birds to quickly replace oxygen in their blood. To avoid a predator, the heavy Impeyan of the Himalayas takes off with a burst of wing beats and glides downhill. It then has to walk back up again.

Young auks →

The Greater Roadrunner does not go "beep, beep". It rattles its bill to make a "clack" noise.

## ▲ Long-distance swimmers

Young auks, Fulmars and Gannets are too fat to fly. They crash dive into the sea from their cliff ledges and swim hundreds of kilometres towards their winter quarters. Constant paddling burns up their fat and, when they are light enough, they stagger into the air.

## TRUE or FALSE?

The speedy Cassowary wears a crash helmet.

# Odd birds

The Kea calls loudly as it soars on mountain winds.

## Fish supper ▶

Many young birds have bright orange or yellow mouths which make obvious targets for their parents to push food into. One adult bird made a mistake, and fed goldfish! A male Cardinal in North Carolina, USA, flew to the edge of a garden pool, chirped, and waited for the gaping goldfish mouths to break the surface.

Male Cardinal

## Meat-eating parrot ▲

The Kea is a fine parrot which lives near the snow line of New Zealand's mountains. It is still largely vegetarian like other parrots, but it has taken to eating carrion and is particularly fond of dead sheep. Because it has a strong, hooked beak, it was thought to be a sheep-killer and was almost wiped out by farmers. Only recent studies of its true behaviour have saved it.

The Hoatzin is also called "Stinkbird" because the contents of its crop – balls of leaves – smell awful.

## ◀A nutty vulture

The Palmnut Vulture – also called the Vulturine Fish Eagle – looks like normal vultures, but actually eats fruit rather than meat. Its main diet is the fleshy outsides of the African oil nut. It is the only vegetarian bird of prey.

It also eats shellfish and hunts for small fish.

## ◀Puzzling bird ▶

The very odd Hoatzin of South America is probably related to cuckoos but its behaviour and body structure are more like a reptile than a bird in several ways. The newly-hatched Hoatzin is naked. If threatened, the young bird will jump into water to escape. It climbs up branches back to the nest, using its beak, feet and unique claws on its wrists. The claws soon disappear. The bird then grows a huge gullet (crop) to store food. Like a large reptile, the Hoatzin gorges itself with food, then has to have a long rest

Nestlings open their mouths wide and cry for food.

Blue-crowned Hanging Parrots roosting.

## Upside down ▶

Hanging parrots go to sleep hanging upside down. In this position they look like a bunch of leaves and must be very difficult for predators to spot. They sometimes hang upside down during the day and even feed upside down.

House Sparrows eating dead flies.

Flies become stuck to the radiator as the car moves along.

## ◀ Meals on wheels

The House Sparrow is very common in cities where it takes advantage of city life. Some House Sparrows have learnt to hop inside the engines of parked cars – they are taking flies off the radiator.

Marbled Murrelet – the small 25 cm seabird is common on the sea.

The Hoatzin is a poor flier.

Young Hoatzin climbing out of the water, using the unusual claws on its wings.

## Nesting mystery ▼▶

Although millions of Marbled Murrelets can be seen on the sea off Siberia and North America, almost nothing is known about their nesting habits. They are often seen flying inland with food but only three nests have been found since the first was discovered in 1931. Two nests were on rocky slopes, one in a felled tree and another, astonishingly, was 40 metres up in a fir tree. The Marbled Murrelet is probably the only auk to nest in trees. Before they can fly, the young of other auks leap from their sea-cliff nests into the sea and swim off. How young Marbled Murrelets reach the sea is a mystery.

# Record breakers

## Flying giant

The Kori Bustard is probably the heaviest bird, weighing about 13-14kg and sometimes over 18kg. There have been reports of a Great Bustard even heavier than this which probably could not get off the ground.

## Years in the air

The young Swift dives out of its nest in Britain for the first time and flies off to Africa. It returns to a nest site 2 or 3 years later, having covered about 72,000km – probably without ever stopping. The Sooty Tern takes off over the vast oceans and continues to fly for 3 or 4 years without ever settling on water or land.

## Great birds of prey

The heaviest bird of prey is the Andean Condor, weighing up to 12kg. The Black Vulture is also very heavy. One female was reported at 12.5kg although they normally weigh less than the Condor.

## Greatest span

The Wandering Albatross has the greatest wingspan of up to 3.7m from wingtip to wingtip. A Marabou was reported with an even greater wingspan of 4m, although most have a span of 2.5m.

## Lighter than a moth

The tiniest birds in the world are some of the hummingbirds. The Bee Hummingbird of Cuba is only about 57mm long, half of which is beak and tail, and weighs only just over 1.5g.

## Deep-sea diver

Emperor Penguins can dive down to depths of 265m, surfacing quickly again, before decompression becomes a problem.

## Toughest egg

Eggs are very strong – a chicken's egg survived a 183m drop from a helicopter. An Ostrich egg will withstand the weight of an 115kg man.

## Great migrations

The Arctic Tern flies 40,000km in its migration from its nesting site and back each year. The Lesser Golden Plover covers 24-27,000km in just over 6 months and flies from the Aleutians to Hawaii non-stop – 3,300km in about 1½ days with over 250,000 wingbeats.

## Most ferocious bird

The most savage and efficient predators are hawks and falcons. They fly fast and when they spot their prey, swoop down and hit it hard with their outstretched talons.

## Largest breeding colony

Up to 10 million Boobies and Cormorants breed together on the islands in the fish-rich currents of Peru.

## Rarest bird

The Kauai e'e of Hawaii, was reduced to one pair in the world by 1980. In America, the Ivory-billed Woodpecker is nearly extinct, if not already gone for ever.

## Senior citizens

A captive Andean Condor, one of the world's largest birds, lived for 72 years. In the wild, a Laysan Albatross marked with a ring, was seen alive and well at 53 years old.

## Speed merchants

The Peregrine may reach speeds of about 250km per hour in long steep dives and, at this speed, a diving Golden Eagle could almost catch it. In level flight their maximum speed is 100km per hour, unless there is a following wind, and they would both be beaten by the White-throated Spinetail Swift which flies at about 171km/h.

## Blurred wings

The Horned Sungem, a hummingbird, beats its wings at 90 beats per second — much faster than most hummingbirds and any other species.

## The biggest swimmer

The Emperor Penguin is the biggest swimming bird, standing up to 1.2m, with a chest measurement of about 3m and weighing up to 42.6kg — more than twice the weight of any flying bird. The Emu is taller at nearly 2m and it swims well although it is a land bird. (Ostriches can also swim.)

## Millions of birds

Of the approximately 100,000 million birds in the world, about 3,000 million are domestic chickens. The most numerous wild bird is the Red-billed Quelea of Africa — there are about 10,000 million birds.

## Largest bird

The world's largest bird is the Ostrich, growing up to about 2.4m tall. Some reach 2.7m and weigh about 156kg.

## The quietest bird

The Treecreeper's notes are so high and hiss-like that they can hardly be heard.

## Dizzy heights

The Alpine Chough has been recorded on Everest at 8,200m and the Lammergeier at 7,620m — both high enough to fly over the top. An airline pilot reported Whooper Swans at 8,230m, which had risen from sea level to hitch a ride from the jetstream winds.

## Largest egg

The Ostrich lays the largest egg — 13.5cm long, weighing 1.65kg. It is equivalent to about 18 chickens' eggs and takes about 40 minutes to soft boil!

## Loudest bird

The Indian Peacock has the loudest, most far-carrying calls which echo for kilometres.

# Were they true or false?

**page 7** The Harpy Eagle eats monkeys for breakfast.
**TRUE.** The Harpy Eagle is the king of predators in South American forests. On its short, broad wings it slips easily between the trees and probably feeds largely on monkeys.

**page 9** After bathing, Starlings dry themselves on sheep.
**TRUE.** Starlings normally dry themselves by vigorous fluttering and preening but a Starling in Shetland was seen to use a sheep as a towel.

**page 10** Bellbirds chime together.
**FALSE.** The Bearded Bellbird does chime like a bell but not in unison with others.

**page 13** Courting pelicans exchange fish.
**FALSE.** Males of many species do bring food to the female during courtship but pelicans have not been seen doing this.

**page 14** Parrots nest with termites.
**TRUE.** Both the Hooded Parrot and the Golden-shouldered Parrot of Australia burrow into termite mounds to make their nests.

**page 16** Hungry young eaglets eat their paren[t]
**FALSE.** The oldest eaglet, however, often kills the younger eaglets and sometimes eats them.

**page 19** Blue Drongos help Chinese fishermen.
**FALSE.** There are several drongos but not a blu[e] one. Some Chinese fishermen use a cormorant on a lead to catch fish for them.

**page 20** The Booby's feet are blue with cold.
**FALSE.** No one quite knows why the Blue-footed Booby's feet are blue, but it is not becaus[e] of the temperature.

**page 24** Swifts fly in their sleep.
**TRUE.** They rise high into the sky at dusk and sleep on the wing, flying down again at dawn.

**page 27** The speedy Cassowary wears a crash helmet.
**TRUE.** The flattened horny crown on top of the head seems to act as a crash helmet as the Cassowary dashes through undergrowth.

# Index